INDIANA CALLING ALBERTA

by
Ethel McKellar

 FriesenPress

One Printers Way
Altona, MB R0G 0B0
Canada

www.friesenpress.com

ISBN
978-1-03-833692-7 (Hardcover)
978-1-03-833691-0 (Paperback)
978-1-03-833693-4 (eBook)

1. BIOGRAPHY & AUTOBIOGRAPHY, PERSONAL MEMOIRS

Distributed to the trade by The Ingram Book Company

Table of Contents

Preface

Many books written, whether true, fictional, documentary, drama, humorous, offer readers a favourite choice. This, my friends and family and all readers, was a dream of mine to write a book. I can honestly say I am not a reader of many books or novels. Once my book is published, I will promise myself I will read my finished script. With pen in hand, this is the perfect time to follow through with my dream. This venture, the journey of my life will be heartfelt, written in all honesty and integrity, and the pure content of my inner soul.

Throughout the content of this book, I will be adding music titles that suit the events and happenings. When you see the quotation marks encasing the song title, please research the song. It will give you a better understanding of the situation. Like in movies, music is a must that draws us into the scenes. Some music titles I have chosen will sound of sadness to bring tears to your eyes, filling the void of loneliness, wanting self-meditation. On the other hand, there will be happy, joyful, and thoughtful love songs that will boost your spirits and make you want to get up and dance. Music in our lives is the best medicine; no truer words have been spoken. All genres for healthy mind, body, and soul.

"Don't Stop Believing" by Journey

CHAPTER 1
Introduction to the Characters

First and foremost, may I introduce myself as Ettie, who solely initiated this composition, this book. "Ettie," meaning myrtle leaf, star, or noble, is of Persian and British origin. It's a diminutive of Esther and Ethel. Whether you're inspired by plants in nature or by the night sky, "Ettie." Baptized apple but nicknamed "Ettie."

Every form of life has a beginning, a presence, and an ending. Somewhat like this will be compiled within this book.

For Ettie it began in Bellevue, Southern Alberta. A coal-mining area, the foraging of coal from 1899 until 2024, which celebrates 125 years in 2024. The start of many mines in the area brought coal miners and families from all parts of the world. Sadly, the worst coal-mining disaster in Canadian history occurred June 19, 1914: a gas explosion that claimed the lives of 189 miners. The mine continued operations until December 2, 1939, when the mine officially closed. Prior to the mine disaster, on April 29, 1903, the Turtle Mountain limestone rockslide occurred, which buried part of the town of Frank, Alberta, killing ninety people. Only eighteen bodies were recovered. In the surrounding area, there were several more mining companies starting up, which created employment to many people living in this area. I lived with this history, looking out our living room window, which faced the Frank Slide. Five smaller towns amalgamated to become the Crowsnest Pass, a well-known tourist destination. That's a little insight into the history of the area. Now onto my personal history.

My father's family was part of the migration to this area. He too lost his dad in a mining accident, and yet my dad, Willie, became an underground miner at twenty years of age and would continue with the trade until sixty-three years of age. He loved playing his accordion for entertainment and for dances. Lived life for the love of hunting and fishing, which this area was very well-known for. Over the Livingston range, not far from where Dad resided, was where my mom, Ethel, was born and raised on a homestead ranch. It's unknown how or where they met, but they fell in love and married in 1945. My dad's favourite accordion tune was "Blue Skirt Waltz," and I'm sure that would have been played at their wedding. They honeymooned for six years until November 15, 1951, when I was born. A second daughter, Darlene, was born six years later, followed by a third, Marlene, three years later. Like a lot of families wanting a boy to carry the last name onward, Dad was a bit saddened, but once he saw we girls could work alongside him like boys, he was more accepting of it.

As my mom's parents were aging, they were needing more assistance with the ranch so Mom and Dad, lock, stock, and barrel, moved us from town living to ranching in the open countryside. Dad continued and commuted to his mining work and Mom helped on the ranch. When the grandparents passed, my parents took ownership of the ranch, and this would be their retirement happy place. Home will always be where one was born and raised.

Us three girls all graduated high school from a small country village school. Now it was time now for us to venture on our own to find our own paths in life. I would join the working force, taking on a variety of employment. Darlene would do the same, and in 1977 she married her soul mate, Paul, who worked for the shell water ten gas plant. They built a lovely new home in the hills, which once was the grandparents' homestead. A couple of years later, they welcomed their first daughter, Dana, and two years later, Melissa was born to complete their family. My sister Darlene will always be remembered by me as a very hard worker, helping on our parents' ranch, raising a family, many janitorial jobs, remembering we were Dad's boys and followed in Dad's footsteps who he too had excellent hard working traits. Living close to my grandparents, it was hard watching them age and fail in health. It was sad when we had to say goodbye to them. Grieving lasted a short while and life moved forward. But our greatest sadness to our family was when sister Marlene, just a year after her high school graduation, was killed in a car accident by an impaired driver. There are not enough words for the hurt of such a foolish act.

"Jesus Take the Wheel" by Carrie Underwood

It was time to get serious. This employment of working at jobs that weren't going anywhere up the ladder and living pay-cheque to paycheque wasn't working. I thought moving to the city of Calgary, Alberta, might be better for job opportunities. As I scanned *The Herald,* a large ad appeared for application for the licensed practical nursing program at Alberta vocational college. Looked very interesting, why not give it a try? So off I went to the information day. That same day, I enrolled to begin my course in January 1978. I believed at twenty-six years of age my maturity, previous work ethic, dedication, and willingness to learn would see me through and that it did. A ten-month course, half would be theory and half would be practical. I surprised myself with how well I did on the written exams and how much I loved the hands-on nursing care. The best day of my life were receiving my cap and certificate. The following month I applied at the Foothills hospital in Calgary and got hired to start my first nursing placement in the newborn nursery ward. There, I would work for ten months.

The bright city lights were not for this country gal. On my days off from work, I ventured home, remembering home will always be where one was raised, to have a visit with my folks. I did that road trip often. While there, I went to a small town called Blairmore and inquired if there were any job openings that I may apply for. The director of nursing asked if I could start the next day. I accepted the job opportunity with the condition that I returned to the Foothills hospital and give two weeks' notice the proper way, which had to be the longest two weeks, like they were never-ending. Yes, I was overwhelmed with excitement for going home, where my heart needed to be.

Happy to be home again and in familiar territory, close to family, neighbours, friends and the start of new nursing experiences at a rural hospital. Within a year's time, a few changes in life would occur. First and foremost, once again helping my folks on the ranch, calling it my base camp. Witnessing the birth of my first niece, Dana Ann, and reacquainting with classmates. If that wasn't enough, helping my folks on the ranch and nursing full time, I took on a casual work as a barmaid at the local tavern. Many folks asked why I placed so much on my plate. With extra funds, I would be able to purchase a newer vehicle. Unreal—I was earning more wages as a barmaid than a nurse. Single at twenty-eight years of age, happy with myself, not really thinking of what might be next to take place. Besides God, there was a pair of eyes watching me: a gentleman named Ken. His construction crew would stop into the tavern for refreshments. Ken kindly introduced himself and drummed up the courage for conversation, small talk, with a twinkle in those eyes that had been watching me. His affection towards me grew stronger and more serious with each chat, which led to a dinner date, which led to a relationship.

My folks were very disappointed by my actions, and we were totally in disagreement with the situation, getting involved with a married man with three children. A heart full of love works in mysterious ways. What captured my heart the most: Ken said his marriage was failing before he met me and said, if it wasn't going to be with me, it was going to be with someone else" I thank God each day that I was the one. My heart, mind, and soul gave me confirmation of this relationship, which in turn gave me deep inner love that I had never felt before then. "More Than a Women to Me" was Ken's song to me. We kept this to ourselves for a very short time, then one day we decided this was cheating and lies, which not only affected our souls but most of our precious dear ones: the children, eldest daughter Connie, daughter Tammy, and son Brian. For both Ken and me, this was an awkward, frightening emotional moment, which in years later become a memorable time. Yes, there were hurtful, saddened, and doubtful thoughts going through their young minds, which were very normal. Children saw me as kidnapping their dad away from them. But as they aged, they had a better understanding of the situation.

Even with a bit of distance in mileage, Ken would always be in presence of their care and upbringing, visiting often, spending time when spare time was allowed, and especially special events, such as graduation from high school. Ask for me, I was so truly grateful when the children accepted me, and my love grew deeper for them. I feel we have a special kind of bond and good rapport, a friendly, harmonious relationship.

Ken was a carpenter by trade, a farm-raised boy who loved horses. He knew wholeheartedly long days of working in the fields, was taught good work ethics that would follow him through life. During Ken's first marriage, he had his own construction company, building trusses, homes, and shops and doing renos big or small. He was building homes in the small village of Lundbreck, Alberta, where we first met while I was continuing my dream of nursing in a rural setting. Following three years of togetherness, we married on July 30, 1982, with three children at our side, and we even took them on our honeymoon.

"Happy" by Pharrell Williams

Ettie of Catholic faith and Kenneth of Protestant faith were married by a Baptist minister. When we get to the pearly gates, we will have choices. "Choices" by George Jones, Ken's favourite country singer.

Together, we decided to remain in Lundbreck, our new forever home. We acquired one-quarter section of land once owned by my grandparents, who homesteaded in the area. Great feeling to be close to family, with my parents living across the creek and road and my sister and her family two miles around the bend. There, amongst the foothills and mountains, we created our own ranch-style living. Both of us continued our nursing/carpentry/ranch-hand skills. This gave the children insight into the country way of life, and many fond memories were made. This area is noted for its great hunting and fishing. For father and son, the joy of hunting was their greatest bond, which would carry on for many years. Saying they lived to hunt would be an understatement. For eleven years we weathered the chinook storms and Pincher Creek and area known to be the windiest place of all of Alberta. With that being said, the wind was a challenge every day, our profits were depleting instead of getting ahead. Time to make a move to greener pastures.

"Four Strong Winds" by Ian Tyson

Leaving the winds behind our backs, we landed in Edmonton and purchased a half section of farmland. Edmonton is a central part of Alberta, rich in agriculture and oil and gas industry. The farm was ideal for our needs. We thanked my cousin and his wife for their direction to this farm, which consisted of exactly what we were looking for. A cozy bungalow for a home, two barns, two Quonset, we fell in love with the farm the moment we drove in the driveway. From seven hours away at the ranch, we loaded up lock, stock, and barrel to move to our new-to-us farm. Equipment, machinery, cattle and personal belongings.

Why, asked many folk, would we want to start all over? Home is where one builds and lives. Within only a few months, we knew we had made the right choice. We loved the surrounding area and friendly neighbours, it was close to the local town that provided us with all agricultural needs, close to my nursing employment and husband's employment at the stockyards. The climate there was very relaxing. No hurricane winds. Both of us were survivors of any storm that presented itself. We never regretted the move to the unknown. Life is what you make of it and what you take away with it. We adapted really well to our new surroundings, looking forwards and not falling backwards.

We spent many labouring hours organizing, building new fences and a new corral system, and erecting a maternity pen for cabin time. The older of the two barns was set up with our new venture in the nurse cow business. What the heck, you ask, is that? A nurse cow is a dairy cow that is not producing the acquired milk quota for the dairy barn production. They are used to coming in line to the barn where they will get a ration of grain once in the station. Instead of being milked by hand or machine, we purchased baby calves, and they do the milking, depending on the individual cow, whether she can feed two or three calves at one feeding. This is done twice a day. When calves reach two hundred pounds, they're weaned and placed on rations of quality feed, then off to the market they go. Then second set of baby calves, only two to each cow, follow the same routine, then cows are given a rest, bread. Once they have their own calf they go back on the milking line. Depending on the age of cow, some will go to the market and be replaced by another nurse cow. We got calls of interest from all parts of Canada, to share the information. We enjoyed this rewarding experience. It's difficult to get away for vacations when one has a farm, with the chores, farming, and processing cattle herd for pasture. It's a 24/7 job. Nice thing is, you are your own boss and make your own schedule. Good thing we could find help for the daughter's wedding weekend.

During these years, the adult children were well on their way to finding their own paths in life. Connie ventured to New Zealand, married her soul mate, Tim, who was a dairy farmer, and they raised three children. Tammy, a dental hygienist, married Colin, and they have one son. Brian is labour worker at various types of employment, has a biological daughter with Christine and two stepchildren. With new found love and wife Darcy has two stepchildren. Extended families are loved just as well as one's own, which I experienced with great love with the three children mentioned above.

One more move on the horizon: Ken's health issues. This would be a good time to retire from intensive labour of carpentry, farming, and manual labour. We moved to the town of West Locke, and Ken found light employment in and around town. Hence the song "Killing Time" by Clint Black. I too was nearing my retirement away from nursing. With my foot care certificate in hand, I started an advanced foot care business, Left and Right foot care, a service in much demand for the elderly and senior citizens. One day, Ken was sitting on the sofa watching television. In my kind, soft voice I asked him if he would consider coming to work with me, in the business. One stipulation: I was the boss! Ha ha. His response was: "I have been the boss for so many years, sure I'll give you a chance," as man and wife working side by side does not work for everyone. Looking back, we were used to helping each other out on the farm. Next twelve years were enjoyable, memorable, and rewarding financially. Many comments from the clients on how well we work together as a team. Clients shared history, stories of the olden days, memorable times, laughter, smiles, and even tears at times. It gave us a sense of pride. Must have been the TLC that gave each individual feelings of comfort. Now officially both retired, ready for some much-needed R&R to enjoy the golden years.

The Golden Years

We cannot go back and change the beginning, but we can start now and change the ending.

Ken and I worked side by side. Together, we achieved the goals of a lifestyle. We gained self-esteem from the country way of life, created memorable moments, overcome struggles the best we could. Forging onwards, our golden ears would be gold and comfortable. Health is the greatest factor. How well people will spend their golden years depends on starting earlier to enjoy those years sooner as there may be roadblocks later. I had only a few minor surgeries with no long-term effects. Besides the changes that come with aging, as I write this chapter, I consider myself fairly healthy. Sure wish there was a cure for arthritis. My dearest husband Ken, a "Man of Steel," was less fortunate. At fifty-six years of age, he was diagnosed with bladder cancer. Thank God for medicine and modern technology. Illness never slowed his pace. Through the years, Ken would be plagued with heart issues, another bout of bladder cancer, and kidney disorders. From three major surgeries, there were long-lasting side effects. With strong willpower and a positive attitude, he always bound forwards, never looking back. Ken stated many a time he was never afraid of dying. It was part of the lifecycle. Throughout the bumps in the road, we weathered the storm, forty-five glorious years together, forever until death do us part.

Ken passed away March 29, 2024.

Debut of Thomas Maquire Martin

I, Thomas, was an only child, born June 24, 1962, to Stoller and Amy Maquire.

I want to take a moment to give you a glimpse of my life in hopes of providing greater insight into the man I am. My dad is an American and my mother is from Lublin, Poland. Both of them met here in the United States. I was born in Arizona where my father came from, but I was raised overseas by my mother's brother and his wife. They took me in after I lost both my parents in a motor vehicle accident. They took me to Poland, and there I was brought up. My uncle married an Indian, so I grew up in a Polish/Indian family. I came back to the United States after college to Texas. I got my BSc in petroleum engineering, spent four years in Poland, and then spent one year in the United States to obtain a master's degree in petroleum engineering. I attended University of Technology, Poland and then got my master's in Texas A&M University. I have been in Houston since 1988. I love travelling, have been to over thirty states in the US, and look forward to travelling and exploring new places. More about my career.

I'm a superintendent in the oil and energy sector, as I do provide onshore and offshore drilling and pressure pumping services. My job allows me the luxury of working from anywhere and I only get to work when I am contacted to do so. I have been in this line of work for twenty years and have worked for several oil and gas companies within and outside of the US. It is a wonderful experience. My previous company was Apache Corporation in Texas. I recently began working privately. I seek contracts from oil companies, get it done, and get paid. It's more aspiring to do something at my very best, enjoying the journey and being happy with the end result. It's also about bringing quality into my life and achieving work-life balance. Helps me appreciate the diversity and commonality amongst us. I am a fun, sometimes crazy, sometimes conservative person who enjoys buying food, movies, live music, dancing, and concerts. I have one of those personalities that allows me to get along with just about everyone. I am family-oriented person and most of all very humble and respectful and a bit shy at times. I have a good sense of humour, have been around happy people that make me smile, and then part with a partner that smiles often. That's a great turn on for me.

Thomas Martin

Throughout this book, Thomas will be referred to as Tom. This gentleman has provided intellectual inspirations on all topics of sadness, loneliness, happiness, and love.

I was living his dream. My career was on the upward bound. Married life was marvellous, and the birth of my son was magical. Over the next eleven years, I continued to work vigorously to strive to a top position, both financially and for my self-worth, enabling me to purchase a home and vehicles and finer necessities without debt for a comfortable lifestyle. The biggest disadvantage was my employment, and contracts had taken me away from home for long periods of time. This placed greater onus on my wife to raise our son alone a lot of the time. The old saying, "You cannot have the best of both worlds," family time and finances. Seems one or the other suffers. Then in a blink of an eye when tragedy happens, our world turned upside down and we were left with broken hearts. Our son was hit and ran over by a careless, underage driver. My world ended. Most sorrowful happening of my life thus far. Which way to turn, how would God heal this hurt? We as a couple had to be strong for each other, together, to overcome this heartbreak, which unfortunately only lasted a short time; neither of us could heal or totally ever overcome the pain and loss. This caused separation of our vows, too much blame placed on each other for why it happened. We parted ways.

There will be painful moments in all our lives that will change our entire world in a matter of minutes. Those moments will change you. Let them make you stronger, wiser, and kinder. Just don't go and become someone you're not. Cry as much as you need to, try to rid yourself of the devil inside, slowly wipe those tears away, straighten your crown, focus, keep moving forward.

"(It Looks Like) I'll Never Fall in Love Again" by Tom Jones

Unless the situation occurs to one personally, there's no words that can explain individual feelings. When inner feelings get a stronghold, there's no letting go. Carry onwards and forwards. (As I continue writing, "we" will refer to Tom and Ettie [myself].) Exchanging heartfelt talks while getting to know each other reduced our stress levels. Never say never that one will never fall in love again. With a different sense of feelings, it does happen. Long-distance relationships do place a damper on intimacy towards two people. Through the Internet, the following notes may row your heart as it did mine. We both at this time were going through sadness, loneliness, and a grieving period via modern technology. Long-distance communications and relations filled the void for both our hearts. Sending to-and-from notes, texts, emails, photos, music, and flowers, sharing loving talks, encouraging each other to find happiness, as the world turns.

A note to the readers, you might find some of the chapters going back and forth, up, and down, inside, and out of context, somewhat like life itself.

CHAPTER 2
Natural Phases

Phases in our lives, as mentioned earlier, include sadness, grieving, loneliness, happiness, and beliefs. Throughout the phases, I will write of my personal triumphs and how I dealt with each one. Opinions are mine and mine alone, as we are individuals, and I cannot assume my thoughts will assist everyone or anyone. We all must come to our own conclusions.

Sadness

In sorrow, hopelessness, heartache, and heartbreak, sadness appears in many ways and forms. The loss of loved ones, especially family and friends, are felt in so many different ways. As children, our first encounter of losing grandparents, which I was told was part of the life cycle. We seem to adapt to the fact faster, as our memories are not as full. Our young minds can easily be rerouted. In our adult years, we witness the loss of our own parents, who have spent a longer period of our lives, which becomes much more emotional. Sadness and subdued times were when our own children had to deal with losing their babies. I turn to God to ask, Why? They have no sins yet. Also, for me was losing my nineteen-year-old sister who was killed in a car accident by the negligence of an impaired driver. To this day I still weep thinking of the tragedy.

I have heartfelt moments of my husband's family members and especially the younger people that left us on this earth way too soon. Death of anyone and anything brings tears to my eyes. Thinking of my longtime animal pets, whether the dog, the cows, or the saddle horse, which passed, but the good times spent with them brings back a smile and positive thoughts. It can be very sad if our intended goals in life are not accomplished and our bucket list is not completed. The greatest fear and sadness: when one's health is failing, diagnosed with a terminal illness. Having been a nurse for elderly residents, most of my career gave me another outlook on death and dying, except when it is your loved one, a much sadder emotional tears your heart apart. My greatest sadness in my lifetime was when my husband, Ken, after forty-five years of marriage, succumbed to his health diseases. Together, we manage the storms to keep healthy as long as possible. Through all the extra hours of personal care, I always loved you. As in the Bible, until death do us part.

"Can't Get Over You" by Lionel Ritchie.
Lyrics of this song will tug at your heart strings.

If you know someone who has lost a very important special person in their life and you are afraid to mention to them because you think you may make them sad by reminding them that they died, you are not reminding them, they did not forget. What you're reminding them is that you remembered that they lived and what a great gift life was.

"Are You Lonesome Tonight" by Elvis Presley

Tears are a way for people to see feelings in your heart. There will be crying throughout everyone's life, not all sad, but there are happy tears of joyful and memorable gatherings and events. We, the human race on the planet earth, will somehow, somewhere be faced with sorrow. I hope others will do their best to overcome our obstacles and be happy once more. Hence the music tune "Happy" by Pharrell Williams.

Grieving

Grief is not a disorder or a disease or a sign of weakness. It is an emotional, physical, and spiritual necessity, the price one pays for love. The only cure for grief is to grieve.

Grief never ends but it changes. It's a passage, not a place to stay. Grief is not a sign of weakness nor a lack of faith; it is the price of love. Grief is like living two lives: one is where you pretend that everything is all right, and the other is where your heart silently screams in pain.

As for my own grief, I was prepared well in advance. It was not a sudden shocking incident when my dear husband passed away. His health issues took their toll over several years, which gave us extra time to accept what the future had in store for us.

Grief, I've learned, is really just love. It's all the love you want to give but cannot. All that unspent love gathers up in the corner of your eyes, the lump in your throat, and the hollow space in your heart. Grief is just love with no place to go.

Even now, as broken as you may feel, you are still strong. There's something to be said for how you hold yourself together and keep moving on, even though some days you feel like shattering. Don't stop. This is your healing, it doesn't have to be pretty or graceful. You have to keep going onwards with the future ahead.

Hey, thank you to family and friends for their great support during my grieving. I was given many suggestions, opinions, guidance, and directions, which were a guiding light to lessen the fears of the future ahead. An asset for sure.

Only in your own self feelings will you find your own way. There are no time limits for we are individuals with our own mindset. I personally do not want to be swayed in a different direction when I have my mind set on where I'm going and how I'm going to get there. Do whatever is best for you—you and only you. You are the only one that has to live the rest of your days, each day for yourself.

When you survive last, everyone is quick to tell you how strong you are, how tough you must be. Actually, no one has a choice to avoid grief, do they? It's not optional. You just have to cry in the shower, sob into your pillow, and pray you will make it.

I am a strong woman!

You never know how strong you are until being strong is the only choice.

Loneliness

Once many tears were shed, I had to face the next phase of loneliness. Another hurt in our hearts. Alone time for me to write a book during this helped me keep my mind occupied with thoughts, ideas, and hope towards positive outcomes. Music helps the soul heal. Now I have a better understanding why my husband, first thing in the morning, turned on the radio. Country music was his favourite. Whatever genre you prefer, the lyrics will heal and fill those empty spaces.

"Only the Lonely" by Roy Orbison

Imagine: Here we are in 2024 still listening to the tunes of the fifties, sixties, and seventies. I believe for me there are the best eras for music for the inner soul. I keep reminding myself I will, I promise to overcome this hurdle. With the next lines, implement them every day, living as soul mates, show your love for each other. I have no idea how to explain to. I only want three things: See you, hug you, kiss you. You are not an option; you are a priority.

Don't wait until later. Later may not happen. Capture those loving feelings now while you have every chance because, like in my case, when your soulmate passes, those moments are lost forever and forever can never be retrieved.

A person never wants to be reminded of *should have, could have, would have* but say the loving words. Deep love makes the heart grow fonder. Try your very best to overcome those lonely situations today and every day.

Heartfelt thoughts when felt from the heart—don't keep them to yourself, in your heart and mind. Let them out, share them with whomever the thoughts are intended for. When you hear that song that wants to make you dance, share it with that special person. Don't wait for later. The meaning will be lost with less meaning both physically and mentally.

Let the love shine on the outside for all to see.

Beliefs

I believe in God and all his creations on earth as it will be in heaven.

Beliefs are individual, personal choices that each of us have within ourselves. You are free to choose but not free from the consequences of your choice. There are no right or wrong choices; it's within your own beliefs. Just follow through in life with what makes you happy and healthy, and gives you peace of mind. We should not be critical of others' choices and beliefs. We ourselves have our own beliefs. Everything will be all right. The whole world, in darkness and trials, is in his caring hands. He's faithful, he's true.

Saying everything is going to be all right, but my circumstances say I won't make it through the night. I need your words to hold me now, need you to pull me through. Having memories today of my dear husband, Ken. I need a miracle, a breakthrough, I need you.

Was told you hold the whole universe in your hands. But my world is falling apart like it is made of sand, and I feel small enough to slip through the cracks. Can you take my broken pieces and put them back together? Give me faith and time to believe you're on my side. Let the past be behind me and the present and future never fail me. Tell my soul all is well.

There's the unknown that silence every fear, there's love that embraces the heartache, the pain, the tears. Through my weakness and my doubting, I hope and pray God's words are unfailing and secure.

At this time of my life, I'm searching for answers for what the future has in store for me, where my next journey is guiding me through for the rest of my life. For some unknown reason, which I have only done once before, I reached out to a tarot card reader. Whatever possessed me of the idea of this is unexplained. Hoping I could clarify and bring my thoughts and doubts of my inner feelings and spirits to the surface, to deal easier with going forward. Wanting the card reader to vision my aura. What a powerful experience! It was totally accurate of my character, my personality, my caring waves, my creativity. A few examples: The reader said I was going to plant a tree. Unbeknownst to him, I had planted a blue spruce two weeks before in memory of my husband Ken. The reader also stated I was taking notes and to continue with the notes and in a few months, I would be compiling those notes. He had no idea I was already writing a book, this book. My cards also said to let that inner child out; now it's time to find a bit more happiness for myself. Amazing! "Seeing Is Believing." Site of where we have been, where we are going.

Back to my story of happiness.

I was the first daughter born for my parents and first grand-child that brought a lot of happiness. Thinking back, I felt the love which would continue all of my younger years. Happy through my schooling days because I liked school and especially the sport of basketball. I was really happy when we won provincials with a great coach. Upon graduation from high school, I remained happy 'cause that segment was completed but just as happy to enter the reality of employment and earning my own way. Greater happiness was when I received my cap and pin from nursing college. My nursing career would span over forty years. I did my best to provide tender care and happiness to the patients and residents of the health-care institutions I worked at. At age thirty-one, once again, my greatest happiness was when I met the man of my dreams, my lover and soul mate. This happiness would span for forty-five years. Unfortunately, happiness lessened as my husband became ill with many health issues, but my devoted love for him would carry me through this difficult time. As a caregiver, I gave him the most comfortable care until his very last breath. God bless.

Now what!? How will I ever regain happiness?

Thank the Lord for family and friends that filled the void of a broken heart.

Still needing and seeking happiness for my inner self.

Music is wonderful to ease the hurt.

"What Becomes of the Broken Hearted" by Jimmy Ruffin

Happiness

"What's Love Got to Do with It" by Tina Turner

Showing love plays a huge part of happiness. From the birth of a child gives happiness of new beginnings. Raising and tending to children, watching them grow and mature, gives joy and fulfillment. Parents fill their children's hearts with love throughout the years. Teens and young adults will create their own kind of love towards each other. Life's next step is to find true love, a soul mate, that they want to share the rest of their lives with, hoping and praying the love for each other continues for many years together. Showing love comes from deep down in the heart, by means of kind and caring words, gestures like hugging, kissing, and touching, and yes, love can also be through material items, such as that box of chocolates, flowers, cards, diamond ring, or a dream vacation. Couples working together with goals in mind will acquire a stronger relationship of love. As we age and look back at the past, love has kept us together, guided us through good times and difficult times. "Good morning" and "goodnight," powerful words. The other day at the shopping mall, it was great to see an elderly couple walking hand in hand, smiling at each other with a twinkle in their eyes. The happiness and closeness toward each other—that's love!

The happiest people I know are evaluating and improving themselves. The unhappy people are usually evaluating and judging others.

Morning is God's way of saying one more time, go make a difference, touch a heart, encourage a mind, inspire a soul, and enjoy the day.

"Happiness" is a powerful word. My thoughts on this segment of the book are my way of expressing happiness. Happiness, I sense, is time spent with loved ones, a true soul mate. "Time is of the essence," a phrase spoken many, many a time. The essence of a relationship, a true relationship, does not happen overnight. It is commutative of communication, caring, intimacy, companionship, deep love, mutual understanding and respect, help and unflinching support. Both should smile together.

"You Can't Hurry Love" by The Supremes

You can't hurry or buy happiness.

The biggest lie we are told is to be with someone who makes you happy. Truth is, happiness is something you create on your own and you should be with someone who adds to it. My way of thinking is, happy soul mates are couples that have similar interests: going places together, doing projects together, even just going for a walk and admiring the surroundings. Most of all, they love being close to one another, hugging, touching, kissing, and letting it show to others.

Togetherness, being on the same page, would greatly deepen and improve relationships. Never lose those loving happy feelings. Happy love requires patience, faith, trust, and loyalty. The chocolates, flowers, and expensive gifts are just added bonuses. You can be happy or miserable—the amount of work is the same. Happiness is wanting and loving what you already have.

Happiness is a choice, not a result. Nothing will make you happy until you choose to be happy. No person will make you happy unless you decide to be happy. Your happiness will not come to you, it can come from you.

"You've Made Me So Very Happy" by Blood, Sweat and Tears

I am so very happy for my closest and dearest friends that have found happiness once again.

"Lean on Me" by Michael Bolton

We are not on this earth to see through one another but to see one another through.

Hopefully, at this point of the book, I have captured your full attention to read forward to reach the ending of my story. I have touched base on life phases of sadness, loneliness, grieving, beliefs, and now happiness. Keeping in mind I speak and write only my opinions throughout, either to be agreed or disagreed. I, in no way or form, want to offend anyone. All statements are my feelings on different subjects. We are individuals with our own thoughts and beliefs. We must not try to change our ways of thinking. We should be supportive, give suggestions, be open minded to our inner feelings, thoughts, ideas, and mindsets. Our individual emotions give us better understanding of someone's mental state at any particular moment, especially through the titles listed above.

"Perfect"—the word used but not all times and things are perfect. We spend a lifetime striving for perfection to reach the pinnacle of what life has to offer. Our most rewarding goal is to do the best, however possible.

Life presents itself with ups and downs, difficult times, hurdles, and obstacles, which we must endure to change times for the betterment of society, to give us peace of mind, so we can look back and say we did that in a positive way. Then there's times we need a little more assistance; we speak to God to guide us in the right direction.

Love

"Love Is All Around Us" by The Troggs.
The lyrics of this song say it all.

Many ways, love can be shown, written with words, spoken, seen, and truly felt. Attaching the word "love" to our letters, messages, conversations, our daily tasks, dreams, actions towards others, our first word spoken as we awake and last word before we retire for the night.

"What a Wonderful World" by Louis Armstrong

Love makes our hearts grow fonder. My own experience when love touched my heart. The most times that would bring tears of joy were when my dear husband said he loved me for the care he was receiving, and when the stepchildren and their spouses say they love me to the moon and back. My heart melts when the grandchildren show their love with hugs, and when I tell my great-nephews how much I love them and they say they love me more, those are times my heart gives a few extra beats. Love is in the air and in our hearts forever. Love can be the creator of peace on earth and towards mankind to enlighten our souls and minds. Let the love flow today and always. The most wonderful place in the world to be is in someone's thoughts, prayers, and hearts. Having someone to protect, care, support, and most of all love us endlessly. Knowing God always answers our prayers beyond our expectations for the very best for our future.

"Lookin' for Love" by Johnny Lee

Is there a right or wrong place? Where two hearts met, forty-five years ago, I met my true love at the local tavern in a small-town country place where folks would gather for socializing.

Folks said this was the wrong place, but their disapproval would be proven wrong. It was the right time and the right place for Ken and me. People meet in church, supposedly a right place. Sometimes yes, this may be partially right but could be with the wrong person. So, our assumptions of right or wrong are that of what an individual assumes. Remember where you met your true love, soul mate, spouse, partner, companion. Could have been at school, university, a workplace, a concert, a grocery store, a swimming pool, a golf range, a clinic, a senior centre, a dating site, or an art gallery. Up north, down South, East Coast, West Coast. Right place, wrong place—it doesn't matter, it's who one meets.

Nobody is perfect.

We all make mistakes.

We say the wrong things.

We do the wrong things.

We fall, we get up.

We learn, we grow.

We move on, we live.

We thank God for always giving us another chance.

Life doesn't allow for us to go back and fix what we have chosen in the past, but it does allow for us to live each day better than the last.

CHAPTER 3
Added Phases of Life: Thoughts, Doubts, and Assumptions

These three titles—thoughts, doubts, and assumptions—will be touched on throughout this book. For better or worse, my intent is for a happy ending. Your personal thoughts are owned by yourself; they are yours and only yours. Thoughts are self-owned. They are produced by your own mind. Created in our brain and self-contained, whether positive or negative, but hopefully more positively for a healthy self-worth. Thoughts run wild at times, so reach out for guidance to change those negatives to positives for betterment in every day you live. Every moment of the day is from thoughts we think of. We start each new day with new thoughts. Let thoughts be your guiding light until darkness ends each day. At times we have second thoughts about actions we take. That is good, so we can make correct choices, not necessarily for others but for your own conscience.

We have doubts and other everyday hurdles that we must analyze closely and carefully. The old saying "When in doubt" is the uncertainty about something. Practise self-compassion, think back to your past achievements, spend time with supportive people, remember you are your biggest critic, seek professional help, and start journaling. May your journey be of a happy ending.

Having unanswered doubts can wear on ones self-worth and self-esteem, health, and mindset. Do your best to clear the doubts. Only you can make that happen; yes, you can. Get support, suggestions, and positive solutions, but only you can clarify those wrongful doubts and wash them away and clean the air for a happy, healthy surrounding. Great values in each of us are important to share with family and friends.

"Criticism," at times, is another nasty word that can be very hurtful in a negative text, or, used positively, can be very rewarding.

If you drink a bit of alcohol, you're an alcoholic.

If you dress up, you're conceited.

If you dress down, you've let yourself go.

If you speak your mind, you are rude.

If you don't say anything, you're snobbish.

If you are sociable, you're a party animal.

If you stay to yourself, you are detached.

Seems like one cannot do anything without being criticized. We live in a society where people are too quick to judge others without knowing the facts. Let's build each other up, be the best we can be, in the same game of life.

Assumptions

Explicit assumptions are those that a person has identified and is fully aware of. Implicit assumptions are those that influence your thinking and behaviours without you being aware of it. Either way humans have encountered both ways of thinking. How we perceive the assumption is how we will react to the statements to clarify either like or dislike. A lot of times, I would agree to disagree, which leaves the more positive spin on issues, situations, and events. We are all individuals. Once again, we assume matters and different ways, but nobody can change our own made-up mind. Our thoughts are totally our very own. Throughout this book I am writing, I cannot really speak the mind of others, so the doubts, thoughts, and assumptions are my personal views. I hope there will be clarification on any concerns toward the ending of my story that will not leave any doubtful negative thoughts, for a happy ending.

Apologizing can be challenging but it's a crucial skill for building and maintaining strong relationships.

Three R's: regret, responsibility, remedy. Regret: *I'm sorry.* Response: I was wrong. Remedy: *Going forward, I'll be sincere, speak from the heart, mean what I say.*

Listen. Hear the other's perspective and acknowledge their feelings.

Be specific. Clearly state what you are apologizing for.

Avoid excuses. Focus on your actions not justifications.

Show empathy. Try to understand how the other person feels.

Follow through. Make amends and keep your promises.

For example, *Hey, Ettie, I'm really sorry for hurting your feelings. I was wrong to do that, and I take full responsibility. Moving forward, I'll make sure our heartfelt relations continue on a happier note. Can you forgive me?*

Remember: Apologizing is about repairing relationships and rebuilding trust. Be genuine, humble, and sincere, and you will be on the right track.

Imaginations and Dreams

What would the world look like or be like without images and dreams? Both keep our minds and souls active for our surroundings to see beauty and everything, in black or white or colour, during the daytime and even at rest at nighttime. Only you can make changes to satisfy your wants and needs to be happy with what you have and your goals and self-esteem. You cannot control how others interpret your actions or words or ways. Everyone perceives things based on their current situation and mindset. Just keep acting honestly, with love and a good heart.

Many books have been written about dreams. Some people dream a lot and some people will have a dream each night as they rest their heads upon a pillow. I can honestly say I live the reality of my dreams. I can awake then go right where I left off and finish the dream to an end, just like the book I'm writing. There will be an ending. Whether it will be a happy or sad, the plot will thicken. Others say they don't remember if they dream or not. Mysterious how the human brain and conscious evolves. An old wives' tale says if you awake from asleep, you should not look out the window first, as that will make you forget the dream you just had. I guess we will just have to try it.

"Dream Lover" by Bobby Darin

This came to my mind today: I must have had a good sleep and a good dream, I just want to get up and dance. Keep the music playing.

Thinking back to my childhood, I had an imaginary friend. Wonder if other or all young girls had that kind of a friend. Was it just a girl thing, a phase we would go through, wondering the same for boys? Did they have imaginary friends? Possibly, or was it the guy thing to do to talk to their car and truck and machine toys, maybe not necessary talking but making all the noises that motors make, zoom zoom.

From young to old, our imaginations are with us a lifetime. We imagine our lives, what should be, could be, would be. Our imaginations run wild to reduce stress, then return to reality. Imaginations can be used to a certain extent for guidance on the correct paths. Give your head a shake to rid yourself of negative and evil thoughts. Letting the inner child out will lighten the mood, improve self-esteem, and will bring happiness and smiles and well feelings.

"This Moment in Time" by Engelbert Humperdinck

Age Matters

Really, does age really matter?! Age is a number from birth till death. Everything on this planet has an age attached to it, whether it is alive, or an object, or an error. Age and time seem to go hand in hand. All life beginnings, learning, maturing, developing will be recorded by age. Life events, ventures, careers, marriages, and families will each have a related number. Personally, just how one presents themselves. We try to achieve youth as long as we can by maintaining health, avoiding medical issues, keeping active and positive thoughts, and holding happiness close to our hearts. As people age, there is no stopping the aging process. There is no cure, but there is control. Another old saying, a play on words: "If you think and act old, you're going to think old." Don't let aging take over your mindset. Keep the child within yourself alive and have fun.

In friendships, marriages, relationships, and companionship, age should not determine one's happiness. Never allow someone else to take your happiness away from you, just because they have their own opinion on your choices you have made. Who are we to judge someone else's age differences? That's totally wrong. My friends, I'm speaking of young, middle-aged, and senior adults. Absolutely no underage children in this context.

We heard it then and we hear it now: what ages males and females are when they meet and get together, males being much older than their mate and vice versa. Remember, it does not matter, it's just a number. It's the love, caring, happiness that we need. All the money or materialistic stuff doesn't necessarily bring joy and happiness.

Just a friendly reminder that all I write are my thoughts and beliefs. Maybe some statements you find I'm painting everyone with the same brush. My true intent is not to come across that way. Please excuse me, and if I sound sinful, please forgive me.

CHAPTER 4
Words with Friends

"That's What Friends Are For" by Dionne Warwick.
Beautiful lyrics that will touch one's heart.

For the past several years, I have not played any games online—actually only three: Scrabble, Wordle, and Words with Friends, which is my favourite. It's my mind therapy. You can play with friends and family, or it can be a chance to meet and chat with new friends. You can choose to play games within your own country or worldwide. This game helped fill the void while grieving for my late husband. Over the years, within Canada, I have gained, chatted with, and acquired new friends. I found this interesting, getting to know folks of all walks of life. I usually don't go beyond my comfort zone. Many people pop up on the screen requesting to play a game, and we have a choice to accept or decline. Many first names appear: Tom, Dick, and Harry or John, Bob, and Joe, to name a few. There is Mary, Jane, and Shirley or Katie, Sally, and Betty.

Maybe that's how Harry met Sally. *The Notebook* movie and soundtrack were awesome.

Nonchalantly playing with my daily Words with Friends (WWF), I accepted a game with Tom. And that, my friends, is how Ettie met Tom. Our song for the movie would be "Amazed" by Lonestar.

I was in Alberta, trying to distract my mind on different thoughts to lessen my sadness and loneliness. WWF was great for that. Meanwhile, Tom from Indiana was on his way to his offshore drilling rig in the Gulf of Mexico. Bear, his operational manager, would suggest to Tom to play WWF for relaxation and to lessen boredom. Neither of us intended to use the game or the chatting as a dating site. Guess what? Much more chatting began as we played our daily word game. Both of us in a lonely state of mind started comparing notes of past and present.

That is when Indiana started calling Alberta via telegram.

I am what I am. I may not be perfect, and I make mistakes, but when I care, I care with all my heart. "Heart" is a key word; we captured each other's heart.

Why me? Tell me it isn't so, it's a dream! You hear the phrase: "You should write a novel." Well, that is exactly what I am doing. Hoping and praying you the reader will follow my journey.

Imagine, if one can fall in love with words alone, how much stronger love would be, like the Bee Gee's say in their song "Words." If you can touch, cuddle, kiss, whisper loving thoughts to each other, holding onto each other, sitting side by side.

Emails, texting, FaceTime conversations—ways for people to communicate—are the new era, and social media. It can be positive or negative. How we utilized these present forms of communication is for us to understand the pros and cons. In conjunction with writing this, a dream love story through only words. How two people can possibly say they're falling in love. Long-distance friendships and relationships can be challenging until arrangements can be made for meeting each other in person, for real, to be able to have a commitment.

Over the next few months, communications lessened as both Tom and I had obligations to attend to incomplete. As for Tom, a two-month contract job on the offshore rig in the Gulf of Mexico was extended because of disruptions of faulty equipment, which halted oil production and extraction. Plans of flying to Alberta to meet me were placed on hold. Patience is a virtue. I was in no hurry to be committed to a new relationship. The loving, intellectual talks with Tom assisted me through my grievance of my dear late husband, Ken. It also brought all the good, happy memories we wanted share to the forefront.

Throughout the first few months of grieving, I felt I was strong enough to see myself through. With family close by and a large circle of friends, I had great support. I didn't need any further counselling assistance. I had Tom's loving positive words to read and listen to, to regain my own inner happiness. I think, at times, we need that outside neutral advice. I have thanked those folks and Tom for their helpfulness to see me through those few months of sadness. The satisfaction I received from family and friends was enough to see me through the tough times. I feel I would not have received the same mindset from counselling or therapy. With that said, that is my own opinion. Counsellors and psychologists are very excellent avenues to go to when we really need, especially with mental health issues on the rise.

"Physical" by Olivia Newton-John

Over a span of only a few months, these are some notes that were sent to me that I could not even begin to reply with intellectual vocabulary:

> I hope you had a good and productive day on your end. I just wanted to rest a bit before writing you this morning and thought I'd firstly update you on my travel ... I got settled into my cabin but decided to relax a bit for a day before starting off work on the machine by tomorrow, which is Thursday. I had a

little issue on my trip when I arrived at the airport with the helicopter that was supposed to bring me to the platform. That was what delayed my movement to the rig until very late in the night after I got the problem sorted out with the company that had to call the airport. I am currently offshore in the Gulf of Mexico. Pretty cold out here and the connection can really be messy and unstable but like I earlier promised, I would always do my possible best to stay in touch. I must confess that, I am so flattered and appreciate all you are able to share with me. I miss you dearly and it's so easy to be able to save it and I truly mean it! You are a very special woman and truly hold a high position in my life now and I can't quite take it in that now that I have found you, we have to be so distant from each other, but I still have faith and strongly believe that our commitments which we share is able to overcome every challenge that's got to come forth ahead of us in life. I am truly blessed, and I thank God for guiding us to one another. Know that you are always on my mind, and I look forward to sorting things out here real quick so we can be much closer to each other soon. *I care for you, Ettie.*

Believing that *you* are mine forever is what makes me get up in the morning. There is nothing I wouldn't do to make *you* mine forever. I am head over heels, deeply and crazily in love with *you*. Thank *you* for giving me the most wonderful days of my lifetime and for making my life most beautiful. *You* are all that matters to me, my love for *you* will last eternally. Making your dream come true is my dream come true, lying in your loving arms is heaven on earth for me. I am never giving *you* up, I'm never ever leaving *you*. Instead, I'll forever and ever love and cherish *you* all the rest of my life, darling. I know that miracles do happen because I met *you*. *You* are simply an angel on earth. Thank *you* for stealing my eyes from the crowd and stealing my heart from me. *You* have sweetened and warmed my life. *You* are the icing on my cake and the heart to my soul. I loved *you* before, I love *you* now, and I will always love *you* forever and ever!

Well, you are the one that needs to go to church today on *our* behalf and thank God for bringing us together because you are way closer to one than me currently, if not I would have gone to church for just today for that purpose, but it seems you don't attend church that often anymore like myself. I feel I've known you all my life because so far we've converse you have always been open and straightforward. That's why I am able to share so much with you in a very short period of time, so I want to use this moment to say *thank* you for trusting and believing in me just as I do the same for you.

CONFESSIONS OF MY UNDYING LOVE TO ETTIE MCKELLAR

(I wrote a résumé for employment at Indiana Affairs. Unfortunately, I did not save it for further reference.)

thomasmartty@proton.me
(Sunday 2024/05/12 @ 5:40 a.m.)

Ettie (My Queen), I just wanted to use this moment to let you know that after reading your résumé for a couple days, you have qualified and beat Indiana

Affairs' expectations, so you are now employed as the queen of Thomas Martin's life. I hope overtime you would deliver and be the best queen to your new employer.

Now let me go straight to the purpose of this mail.

Was thinking about you and us yesterday so I took my time to type this out for you:

While most of the joy we get in our relationships comes from being together in person, there are times when we need to think of our future before we can enjoy the present. These days, it's absolute misery knowing I can't be where you are, and you can't be where I am. But despite this, I know that this momentary sadness won't last long. Sooner or later, we will find the right moment to be together. And when that time comes, nothing in the world can ever tear us apart. I love you and I'm proud to say it, I miss you, and I want you to always have the courage that surely, we will be together soon and forever my queen.... .

For anything worth having one must pay the price, and the price is always hard work, patience, love, and self-sacrifice. Babe, we're sacrificing the present for a better future (which has always been a work in progress in our individual lives). We're working now so that we can relax and be happy and content in each other's company in the coming days. I know that it's hard for you and me to not be able to hold each other whenever we're feeling down and low. But remember that I am just a phone call away (and even when I am not, that doesn't mean I am far from your heart because I am always closer to you if you could only look within you for my reach inside you an power of love that's proved to be so magical indeed). Text me and I'll always be there. Call on me and I will be there with you to lend my ear and soothe you with my voice and comfort you in spirit, body, soul, and mind. I am there with you all the way, and nothing can get in the way of that. At every given chance I get to share those enjoyable and memorable moments with a woman of my life, my long heartbeat, my one and only sexy queen.... .

These days all I can do is think about you while working and my off-duty time being all alone makes me reminisce about you but why is that, babe? You complete me as a man. Before I met you, I already thought I was content in my life. But I finally learned what I was missing when you came into my life. I now can't imagine a life without you by my side. I can't imagine what happiness can be if you're not in the centre of it all. I look forward to all the big things we'll do together like travelling, visiting the ranch on a favourable weekend weather. I also look forward to the little things like cuddling up on the couch, falling asleep in your arms, going on fun dates and just talking about anything and everything. I even look forward to days when we might not be in such a great mood and are arguing, only if that will make our lovemaking even sweeter. Babe, while you may be a bit far away from me, you're always in my heart. I keep joy here as you keep me in yours. I love you more than the distance that separates us. We both know that this separation isn't permanent, but the best part is that we're only spending time apart so that we can finally unite in person 'cause I bonded with you spiritually, that simple, due to the fact that I feel your presence around me even though I can't touch or feel the warmth of your body yet. Once I picture your face, I just feel your present instantaneously and never be apart.

As I read these paragraphs that were written by Tom, I hope any or everyone reading these will be having a very warm, enlightened feeling. I think all people, no matter age or ethnicity, need to hear verbal statements more often to create more loving thoughts. We tend to get too involved with everyday routines, tasks, and schedules. We lose our loving part of life. As the saying goes, "Life is too short."

REASSURANCE OF MY UNDYING LOVE/TRUST FOR OUR UNION

(Words from Tom's online communications with me.)

I just want to reassure you of the love and trust I have for you that seems to grow much stronger and everlasting each passing minute of the day and also show my appreciation for all what you've done to and for me in the course of our relationship so far … honey, I am glad that you came into my life. I have always wanted the love of my life to be understanding, loving, caring, faithful, and most of all someone who would accept me for who I am and have the desires and passions to want to have me always as much as I want you babe. Now I have found the person I was looking for. My heart told me that my "Queen Charming" was there when you first responded to me on WWF. I didn't have to think twice to extend a hand of friendship towards you and ever since then my feelings and perspective of you and your rare personality has grown so further and I knew that you were Mrs. Perfect for me. I don't think that there is, or there could be, anyone better than you out there for me that could be able to replace such unique true love you've showered on me and this has inspired me to submit myself to you completely and love you with my whole heart because you're indeed all I've ever wanted in life to make me complete in more ways than one and I will never love anyone as much as I am going to keep on loving you because there's truly no space to do that in my heart for anyone except my most loving and sexiest 2H2H.

I mustn't forget to add here the dream I had about us last night: I saw you on the pier, the wind was blowing through your hair, and your eyes held the fading sunlight. I was speechless as I watched you leaning against the rail. You are beautiful, I thought as I saw you, a vision that I could never find in anyone else. I slowly began to walk towards you, and when you finally turned to me, I notice that others had been watching you as well. "Do you know her?" they asked me in jealous whispers, and as you smiled at me, I simply answered the truth: "Better than I know myself." And then as I moved closer to you, I stopped when I reached you and took you in my arms. I long for this moment more than any other. It is what I live for, and you when you return my embrace, I give myself over to this moment, at peace once again. I raised my hand and gently touched your cheek, and you tilted your head and closed your eyes. My hands were hard and your skin was soft. As they reached out to kiss your smooth lips so passionately as they taste so much like strawberry fruits and I just wanted to eat them up with mine (I can almost feel you beside me as I write this email, and I can smell the fragrance of your love. I am trying to hold onto it though). It was as if sparkles of lights were dancing between us and we couldn't stop and contain ourselves by just looking at one another. Our heartbeats beat as one since our hearts have already been united by a union that only eternity can sustain and at that moment, I just wanted more and more of you and just prayed in my heart that you'll never have to leave my side no matter what happens in our lives... .

Now that you are already a part of my life, I thank the Almighty God for blessing me with such a wonderful creature like you. You have changed a lot of me with your wonderful person. You fired up my dry spirit and brought fresh water to my thirsty heart and soul. You coming into my life has ignited a certain passion in me that has never been there before. Reading your messages and emails rekindled my dull moments and brought lights up my day. Oh, my queen, how I wish that you are here with me. But even though we are a distance apart, in my heart, soul and mind you're always here, alive, breathing, and touching my life with a million positives ...

Often, I pictured us holding hands and watching movies on the couch together, sitting on beaches and watching the sun go down in the stars come out, sitting beneath old oak trees, Anne listening to songbirds singing, and hearing you laugh through-out the day and dreaming of catching you smiling at me when you thought I didn't see. And all I can do is hope that when you close your eyes at night, your mind is filled with thoughts of me. When we fall asleep, can we dream together, no matter how far apart we are? I went to sleep thinking about you, and I woke up just the same. And you know, you're my favourite reason to lose sleep—don't you?

Sometimes I am lying in bed with nothing but the idea of you and me. Right now, you are asleep, but oh how I wish I was there. Stroking your back and running my fingers through your hair. Our legs tangled together beneath the sheet, as I gently traced my fingers along your lips while counting each and every eyelash. And there's so many things I could say to you about how I want to make plans for just you and me. And how when I look at your picture, I see this person who makes me realize all the things I've wanted for so long. And I know you're miles away, but I promise, even if I have to walk through all your dreams, I'll be seeing you soon and loving you even more. More please.

I, Ettie, am in awe, speechless, heart pounding, for how could one not love these words spoken? My reply once more: Tom, you should be writing a novel of love.

CHAPTER 5
Promises, Plans, and Personalities

Personalities: individual mindsets, whether acquired through hereditary traits, learned by one's surroundings, adapted by social contacts. Once achieved, a person will carry own personality throughout life. Some personalities may be changed if they are unacceptable. In some cases different personalities attract one another. Maybe so, but two people in a relationship with similar personalities will share same interests, which can be very beneficial to be happy spending time together.

As for Tom and me, two people from different walks of life, different backgrounds, making their talks and sharing notes very interesting and making an effort to see the other's way of thinking and perspective. This made for many texts to and from each other, another important way to get to know someone from the first encounter and still very much the unknown of each other. Over a short period of time, we each became more comfortable, opening up our minds and hearts for one another. At times, we truly felt we had known each other for a long time, which led to trusting one another's plans and promises, setting goals for a healthy and happy relationship. We had many talks in agreement, so as a couple we were on the same page of thoughts, likes, and dislikes. Oh yes, there were talks in disagreement that would have to be clarified with one another before any further moving forward could take place. My feeling was to overcome the hurdles from the beginning before they became a mountain to climb. Rid those challenges before thoughts and feelings scarred for life. I would like to send this message to all folks for betterment of a loving and caring relationship.

"Communication," a very powerful word. At the present, near future, and always. Without good communication, a damper will be placed on one's daily thoughts and feelings. Left unresolved, the levels of communication lessen to the point that people become distanced from each other. This is not good, for the loss happiness within our souls is difficult to regain. Any person strong enough to know the lack of communication is happening, nip the situation in the bud, seek help before it festers to the point of no return. True love is good communication.

Promises Made and Debts Unpaid!

I, Ettie, make sure that my promises were met. First and foremost were to my folks to live by their expectations, which included staying away from troubled, difficult situations, be kind and caring to all mankind, to get educated and be self-sufficient, make good and proper choices. My promised marriage vows to husband Ken of forty-five years was to love and cherish for richer or poorer, through health and illness, till death do us part; that promise was fully fulfilled. My lists of examples of promises overtime were also done. If I promised to help my cousin's wife with country chores, take nieces on a holiday, share my garden plants, give a friend a treasure of mine, help a senior neighbour, take care of grandchildren, even a coffee visit or phone call with a dear friend, I tried my darndest to follow through. Oh yes, for unforeseen reasons some promises were not met, and these ones still haunt me. There are reasons for which at times are out of our control and realizations. I believe promises are goals we place upon ourselves to strive towards, to make us feel accomplished.

Tom, on the other hand, had many promises, whether they were to himself or to me, kept or unkept. Many a time his promises to himself were for the betterment for a happier mental state, to forget the past and move forward, to continue to make his dreams come true. "You can promise someone the world"— again an old saying too often said but not completed, unrealistic. As our friendship continued, Tom made materialistic promises, which at this time were very overwhelming, which also made my heart beat a little faster. Reality and seeing is believing. Promises are just promises if not fulfilled. At this stage, our friendship was turned into talks of a relationship, plans for the future as a couple.

"From This Moment On" by Shania Twain.
Beautiful, beautiful lyrics.

The Promise Land

"Promise to Love" by Kem, a song sent to me from Tom.

Three words, "I love you," I promise you used most frequently written or spoken to each other in vows of marriage for couples, expressed to family members, friends and children. Those words say so much to tell true meaning from your heart and your inner feelings.

Tom said, "You know, you've completely changed my life in every way, inside and out. When everything wasn't in my favour, you stepped in and made everything better for me and unconditionally changed me with lots of positivity. I love you so much and if any day I have to sacrifice my life for you then I possibly will do that. You make my heart beat faster than ever. I love the way you take care of me. Those make my day. And all your activity makes my heart just melt to love you."

The next day I received this note from Tom:

I can't stop loving you.

I have to be honest I think about you a lot.

In the morning and at night and the middle of the day it's all you.

I can't think of a better way to spend my time.

I'm crazy about you just know I gave you my heart and I don't regret it for a minute.

Tissue time! And once again I stated to Tom that he should write a novel of love, to encourage people as they need to hear such words like this more often to lighten their love life and keep bringing the loving feelings to the surface.

My thoughts were running wild and wishing I could have done more also in the past years, but not holding onto just thoughts but actually following through with my thoughts. A positive note: My personal thoughts, as I'm writing, keep my mind active and vivid. This next segment reaches out to marry couples, whether one year, ten years, twenty years, or forty years, for relationships, friendships, companionships, to keep the level glow and alive. Small gestures do not have to be huge to show you still loving each other. For the female, one shares their love with flowers, sweets, jewelry, clothing, a new sweater, or a household item or a date night. For the male, from the hardware store a new tool he says he would like to have, a new hat and gloves and let's not forget a new tie, or a surprise of a favourite dinner and an evening. Yes, these are material ways. How about notes left on the table or kitchen counter, by the remote control, on each other's desk, on the pillow when one awakes, and nowadays using text messages during each other's workday. One can send a song and lyrics with captions poems, photos, all to send to one another the loving feelings towards one another.

I fell into a scheduled routine way of life, at times, saying I was too busy. Today, I dislike that word, "busy." A person should take time and make time for those precious moments for happiness throughout the days, weeks, months, and years. The old sayings, "We're only going through this life on earth once," and "What we missed today can never be replaced." Let's rejoice and create a happy place in our lives. Amen.

> Reassurance of our love, today, a smile should appear on your face. It's because of you, at this very minute, I am thinking of you, and I am smiling too. Thinking of you makes my life complete. You're my golden clouds, you're my smile. You are all the soulful love songs within my spirit, like an angel calling me ... Perfect for my soul. Thoughts of you warm my heart like a moonlit summer night. You are the one who makes me feel happy every day. You make me feel this great and nice, genuine passions in my life. Hope you know what it took me in writing you this lovely email today, because you are the joy in my heart. You complete me, my wife forever. In my thoughts of you there is an underlying love that is present in every word, every glimpse I hope you feel it as I do, for it is what I am and ever I will be for you, babe. I am thinking of you, in my sleepless solitude today and I know that if it is wrong to love you, then my heart just won't let me be right. 'Cause I'm drowned in you, and I won't pull through, without you by my side till eternity ...

What if "we" is the answer and love was the question? What if all this time it was "us" you were supposed to find? I am filled with wondering questions and doubt, but of one thing I am most certain of, it will always be you that gives flight to the butterflies inside of me, come to the sea I have become and hope to the darkness all around us at times. It is you and it has always been you. You that excites and spreads joy like rainfall on the already damp earth. You that pulled me from the longest sleep and kissed my tired eyelids awake. If life is a question mark, then you, my love, are the proud and bold. That is typed with certainty at the end of my rainbow. Because of you, half the time I don't know that I'm smiling but I am. One of the best things I do during my day when I'm thinking of you is listening to my heartbeat and knowing that it's beating like that because of you. Because of you I can feel myself slowly but surely becoming the me I have always dreamed of being. Because of you, I laugh a lot more, cry a lot less, and smile a lot more.

I fell in love with you because of a million tiny things you never knew you were doing. I find the most beautiful moments of life aren't just with you talking and texting to me every day, but because of you, and I can't wait to tell the world about our insane love affair ... Only if you agree that is ... lol! Last night I hugged my pillow and dreamt of you. I wish that someday I dream about my pillow, And I'd be hugging you—I miss you so much! I miss you a lot more than I realized in these past few weeks. Things keep happening and I always find myself wishing I could tell you about them right when they happened, but I know that isn't possible.

You make me happy. It's the kind of happiness that only comes from love. The kind that gives you that tingling feeling in your stomach and shivers down your spine and then you stop and think, How did I ever live without this? In your dark days, just turn around and I will be there. And maybe I won't have any more light to give you than what you already have, but I will take your hand, and we will find the light together. Please don't ever leave me, babe. Without you, there is no me. You make me happy in a way no one else can.

For me, there is only you. My heart for you will never break. My smile for you will never fade. My love for you will never end. I love you. You're like the love of my dreams, but better. I can't stop thinking about you. It's you, babe. Because no one else makes sense or meets my standards of what I call a real woman, but you do. Each day may fade, but my love will continue in every way. You are every reason, every hope, and every dream I've ever had ... And to say "I love you" now and when I'm way older ...

I don't think I've done justice telling you how much I love you or how much you mean to me, but there are many years ahead for me to get my message across and make you the happiest woman on earth. I cherish every moment we have together even if it's just a quick phone call, email, or text message. The sound of your voice reassures me that everything is right with the world once again and I can breathe a little easier knowing you're safe and out of harm's way.

So, take my hand, and with it comes my heart ...

My soul … my love. My trust … my faith. My hopes … my dreams … my past, and my future …

So, take my hand and with it all I have … all I am … Is forever yours .

As I continue writing this book, I have gone over and reread several times the emails that were sent to me from Tom. His writing was very intellectual to voice his feelings and thoughts. in comparison to my words. Mine were very simple, common, everyday words. Guess whichever way written, we got our messages across to each other. The main goal was to keep connected and stay in touch to support each other through our journeys.

We lessened our emails to and from and began texting back and forth. Only a few actual phone calls were made. Tom said from the first phone call we got our laugh back again. We had motivation to get our lives back on track and our problems didn't seem so bad. With texting, it was instantaneous communication to encourage each other to have a good and productive day. Just when things seemed to be going well, problems started. Tom had some setbacks and hurdles on the offshore rig platform and with access to his funds. Tom helplessly asked for a small amount of financial help as a temporary investment, with promise to refund me once back on shore in Indiana. I took the risk and trusted him, but he would honour his promise of payment . kind of like going to the casino: one takes their chances. Our chats were less as Tom was very preoccupied with his contract and job. As for myself, I too was busy organizing a memorial for my dearest husband Ken to be held July 30, 2024. I was also involved with organizing a hometown reunion to be held September 6, 2024. Many tears were shed, both sad and happy, at those two events.

In Tom's words:

DO NOT ALLOW OTHERS TO TAKE AWAY YOUR HAPPINESS

Babe, to be honest, I'm not one who'd pretend to be someone or something that I am not, and too old to play such games with you either. Trust me, pain is no stranger of mine and I'd hate to cause you any. I know what it feels like to be broken because I have been broken. I have given my time, my all, my money, my love, my heart, mind, body, and soul to someone just to have it thrown back in my face. I loved someone with every ounce of my being and had them turn around to betray, like, take advantage of me, and break my heart more than I ever knew was possible. I have been scattered into a million pieces and had nights where I would look at myself and think, Where do I even start putting myself back together again? But then, I decided that just because I was broken didn't mean that I had to stay broken. I know that life is hard and it's always going to throw hurt my way and I know that sometimes life just sucks, and it feels like you can't catch a break no matter what you do. But you fight, and you try even when you think you have nothing left to give, because that's all we can do. It's the only thing we can control. We can't control if other people heard us, and we might never know why. I believe that there are really sad people in the world, but I also believe that there are some really good people out there too. If you just take the time to look, even if you have to look really hard, I believe that love does exist and it's worth it to take the risk. I have been there before and got through it. The best thing that can happen, is you find the love of your life and that's not worth fighting for, then I don't know what is, babe. I love you.

Yours truly, Thomas

CHAPTER 6
Mind over Matter

Our minds are the generator of our reactions. What we absorb, what we feed into our minds will produce our own individuality. For better or worse, oneself is the deciding factor for what path to take. My subconscious was lurking around the edge of uncertainty. Although my friendship with Tom was at a trusting state from our conversations, in the back of my mind I still had doubts, accusations if this situation was for real. At this stage before any more commitment, I needed more concrete answers to feel safer. Tom was wondering why so many questions and disbeliefs with his replies, "I've invested my time and my heart and my feelings my love into us. I cannot call it quits no matter what may happen." I began more in-depth research of Tom. I was told from the beginning that he was a subcontractor for Conoco Philips on an offshore rake platform in the Gulf of Mexico. He gave a phone number but was unable to get in touch most of the time because of the poor reception. FaceTime and video calls were prohibited for security reasons. I asked Tom his home address in Bloomington, Indiana, jokingly, saying to him I was going to meet him there when his contract was completed. Not really; the plan was for him to come to Alberta. So I never did get an address. Tom texted and said to me, "Reduce your thinking rate because I feel you're just being too anxious for no tangible reason. Take out those negative thoughts."

Elvis Presley's "Suspicious Minds" was written for both Tom and me on this path for the future. Almost every day I would receive a text, a song, a picture of a bouquet of flowers to lighten my dark, dampened thoughts. But still in the back of my mind, I could not rid myself of disbelief of the situation that surrounded me. As my plot and doubts thickened, I felt more at ease with a clear mind to ask Tom more direct personal questions and deeper feelings for me. Some answers I heard were repetitive, excuses distracting from the truth—almost to the point of what I would call red flags. Be cautious, be careful, my subconscious was speaking to me.

Once again, I went through the phases of life for no more mistakes to be made by myself. I was saddened once again, knowing this friendship was going to resolve with a forever ending. Tom replied, "Wise, after all our loving conversations that I sent, you still are not really in a happy place. Ettie, you have had many bouts of sadness, which you have overcome, many times laughter came from those talks." Tom said to me, "I'm supposed to be your personal trainer, advisor, entertainer, comedian, and provider." My thoughts began to turn to negativity, which Tom sensed immediately and said he didn't know why. I wanted to find someone nearby when I already found him.

I voiced my assumptions, how I really felt, wanting straightforward, truthful answers. Tom's reply: "Please don't make such assumptions jokingly because my emotions are fragile so when you say such things like that, I feel offended so stop making such insinuations."

At times, during the few disagreements, Tom's attitude changed during our texts. I, as the type of person I am, would apologize for hurt feelings. Tom said he didn't need my apologies, and to keep them to myself because saying stuff without consideration would hurt his feelings. At certain points like this, I think we were losing our loving feelings for one another. During our downtime talks, I chalked it up to getting to know each other. Nothing is perfect. I believe a lot of relationships have these times, where good communication will get you over these hurdles. What we must do is rid ourselves of grudges that would fester good times in our union. Resilience has to be for both sides, for happiness to continue. Still, at this point, our friendship had many unanswered questions. Some wounds have healed but some hurt cannot be fixed or wiped clean from the slate. We needed more time, whether this love story was going to have a happy ending.

I sent this: "Hello, Thomas, if this is you for real let me know or how someone taken your identity, would love to still talk just like we did on WWF."

From Tom:

> Things may seem unstable and sketchy a bit right now because of the situation here but honestly, there is one thing that will never change and that's the feelings I have for you, it will never fade or go away. You may have been told some ****** things about me from people who do not even know me or have spoken with me in person or otherwise (it's crazy). I love that you don't judge me based on my situation, please don't, my sweetness. I have loved you for you and not for what you have. I want you to know that running to you for help wasn't an easy decision on my part, I had crisis with myself before I could bring myself to ask you to help me out because I am not the kind of man that would rather ask of his woman instead of assisting his woman. I want you to understand the situation I was facing on ground right here

is a big mess and could mess up my life. Not only have I invested too much in this contract, if eventually the contract clauses breach, the contract can be terminated. If that happens, it would be so painful that I have to lose my money, my effort, and all I've invested in the contract so far and all I've worked for. I just want you to know that I love you until the day after forever. I will always be around for you. I love being loved by you and I never want it to end. I understand that love is so strong yet so delicate, it can be broken, to truly love is to understand this! To be in love is to respect this. The best and most beautiful things in the world can't be seen, nor touched, but are felt in the heart. I know love is a precious gift! The small things that are more precious and meaningful than all the riches of the world. The love I have for you cannot be quantified with any amount in the world and I'm not just saying this. I love you and I'm not ashamed to say I love you helplessly. Please listen to the song below, it's my promise!

"The Promise" by Tracy Chapman

Yours truly,
Thomas

Once again, my mind was running rampant with negative thoughts. Too many unanswered questions, having second doubts about long-distance friendships, relationships, and companionship, especially from another country or far distances. During my happily-ever-after marriage of forty-five years, the three mentions above never entered my mind. They don't for people until they experience separation or divorce or lose a loved one. I think companionship is the most popular avenue people may follow.

My take on companionship is that it can be ever rewarding for two people to have happiness for the rest of their lives and their onward journey in life. Happiness to each individual person varies to one's choices, intense characteristics. No one person can voice to anyone else how they should live in harmony. There are no set guidelines, rules, or regulations to follow to create a new companionship. It is only between two people who have found each other. In some cases, a second chance for both. As for me, at this time, my own doubts became clearer. I had chosen the wrong path and realized distance does not make the heart fonder. In my case, there were too many obstacles to overcome, and I have become a stronger person from my weaker mental state.

Thank God I realized I needed some neutral assistance for a choice I needed to make. Thank you so very much to two ladies, names withheld for confidentiality reasons at this time. Thanking you both for your kind, private understanding and guidance. You both have my permission to introduce yourselves once the book is written and published.

The story of Tom and Ettie does not end here. We continued our conversations with cooler feelings towards one another. Several days and weeks would pass before we texted. I still needed more questions answered, and replies from Tom were still heart-felt, influential. I straight away asked if he was Thomas Martin or did someone else steal his identity using his photos, information, and history. Because this, we know, happens. Was I so naive not to see the signs? This might have been the situation. We talk about hindsight. Maybe I see it now. Why me? Tom's reply to that statement was: "Because you think you are not enough. Why not you? Yes, now I should be feeling bad for letting my heart choose you amongst the zillion others that you're referring to."

Who would have thought by just an honest simple word game on the Internet, one could be captivated into a disrespect-ful situation. Even though by this time I knew what was taking place, I continued with questions in hopes of getting a confession and truth to who the real Thomas Martin was. Are you the true Thomas Martin I have photos of? Are you truly a petroleum engineer? Are you going to keep all those wonderful promises? Or are you using someone else's identity? Are you a scammer? Have I been talking to a robot? Once again, the reply was: "I really don't understand you at times, why you choose to doubt me. Why do you keep saying things like this? You hurt me very deep without knowing. I overlooked some things just to prove you wrong. I'm a lover, not a fighter for people I love. I'll fight to defend them to my last breath."

Whoever you are, wherever you are, I would like to thank you for your inspirational conversations. Even after I finally realized I had been scammed, I continued for a short while gathering info for my own use and maybe a confession from the alias, Thomas Martin. With photos only to go by, I would love to contact that person and tell him his identity has been stolen.

My warning to everyone: Please be vigilant of your surroundings in this cruel world we're having to deal with. We, the honest people, can easily fall into traps, be strong to reverse terrible situations. Finally, it came time to read and delete all texts, conversations, and contact sites and any connections. Oops, I forgot the email address, which led to one more email from Tom and here it is. Really, still in awe of whoever wrote these scripts. "Unbelievable" was my reply.

> A small mistake of mine has ruined our relationship and has made us feel sad. now, please forgive me and help me get everything back to normal . as you have said and I have as well, nobody can be perfect. Each one of us has flaws. I made mistakes that disappointed, I am guilty of what I have done. I beg your forgiveness. You are a person with a big heart. I love

you even in times of challenges like this. I always cause some mess. It is never your fault. I'm sorry for making you feel unhappy. I cannot believe that I cause hurt to you. Since the day I met you, you fill me with all the unconditional love and care. I left your heart full of hurt. Still, you fill my life with all the nice things I can see, but I filled yours with cries. Babe, I am asking for your forgiveness. With you I have learned to just let my feelings out when my heart is about to burst because I know now that you won't judge me or put me down or think that I am a silly man. I can now find the strength to untame my feelings when I used to be afraid of saying words or how you might perceive them. When I've been feeling down or had heavy feelings welling up in me, you take me from my dark place, and I feel the warmth from your soft and warm arms around me to keep me steady so that we don't fall apart, and you are always there to catch me from falling. I feel you close to me and protecting me with your soft words of encouragement to stay with you because you tell me everything is going to be all right, and then it is, and then I feel the anxiety wash out of my body call my mind and heart and I'm at peace again. I have *never* (there is that word again) had anyone care enough or be woman enough to cry with me, comfort me, and soothe my aching heart like you have and there are not enough words to express how good that makes me feel, how close that draws me to you, and binds our love with one more tie. Lastly, how appreciative I am that you have the power over me. When I say those three words in the beginning, that gave you pause, I really hadn't experienced the kind of love that you have shown me and showered me with. I just thought I knew what love was until I met you. Your kind of love is not even describable in words, but I will spend the rest of my life trying to find the best way I can tell you, but even better than that, I will show you rather than say it once I'm out of here. I feel like I'm ready now for the "Ettie-Thomas kind of love" that every little boy dreams of having, about their Princess Charming that came from a small town not too wealthy who doesn't wear expensive clothes but still has the charming and cute smile and beautiful voice that sings them to sleep every day and night, and which made us swoon at the movies or when we read love stories. I want to be your everything and more. I know it's often that you say "I love you," but I just want to be sure that I'm yours and your mind forever and ever. I may need your reassurance from time to time more than you know because I am so overwhelmed with your love for me, that sometimes I feel like I'm in a dream and I'm going to wake up and it was only that, a dream. I know you may not be able to understand this feeling I have at times, but I'm trying to express how deeply in love I am with you, how committed I am to you, how you take my breath away (a way like when you write me something beautiful like I received from you time to time), and quite honestly, I never want that or this to end—*ever!*

That email would be the last email I accepted from Thomas Martin. My last words to this story were a learning curve about scammers and to whomever reads this book that you too have been warned and informed and to be careful so that you never get trapped in a similar awful situation as this. When in doubt, seek help. Research any unknown scenarios and people when you feel any uncertainty.

DELETE, DELETE, DELETE!

My case has ended. If Indiana is calling Alberta, I'm not home. Thank you and goodbye. Oh no.

CHAPTER 7
Silence of Scammers

This chapter will reveal my personal experience of being scammed. I despise the word "hate" and more so despise the word "scam." A much softer word would be "dislike," and it will be used to distance ourselves from the word "hate." I might have lost your attention, but readers should be informed of the risks of scams.

There is and has been a lot of information given to us, the honest people, via news media, workshops, speakers at conventions, at seniors' facilities, posters, libraries, emails, and help lines.

Anyone and everyone is at risk, regardless of age, ethnicity, or gender. Scammers pray on only the lonely, grieving, vulnerable, naive, and careless people; this is an understatement. Everyone on this planet can be put in harm's way. Companies, businesses, churches, sports groups, even secured authorities are at risk.

We have to be more diligent of the dishonest people that surround us. Never accept the unknown. When in doubt, seek help from family members, loved ones, or law enforcement. Scamming is worldwide. Our society has changed. We the people have to make personal changes to protect ourselves. We know in the advanced technological world that if we use devices like computers, cell phones, tablets, and laptops, we have to be careful not to tap the wrong button or never give the unknown personal information. When in doubt, delete, delete, delete. Please folks, take heed to our crazy, cruel world. I hope and pray you do not get drawn into the same situation that I have encountered. Sure was a learning curve for me and hope I can advocate from my awful experience.

Over the course of four months, I heard many personal stories from family, friends, and acquaintances. As stated earlier, I dislike the word "scam," but will used "scam" for this section as folks have voiced their stories and encounters of being scammed. As I listened to the stories, it was all I could do to keep silent on these matters as I was in the midst of one myself. On the plus side, I was gathering information from the various stories for context for this book. Sleepless nights—oh yes, not only of the grieving of the passing of my beloved husband but also from stress of being scammed. Hindsight, those might have been the factors for sleepless nights and fatigue. Oh yeah, I was given a lot of ways to overcome my state of affairs but in my heart, mind, and soul, I will get to my happy place once more. I'm just about there as I write this chapter.

Folks, you might have seen I was a bit out of sorts at times. I knew myself that I was. Yes, it was difficult to keep the secrets only to be read in this book. I managed to rectify my mistake and survived.

Scenarios of Scams

Scam encounters are worldwide, in your own country, cities, towns, and neighbourhoods. No true scenarios, no names mentioned for confidentiality.

The other day at our local bank, two young ladies were having funds deposited to their bank account from an unknown person. The bank teller, several times, stated this transaction was a scam. I cannot say what the outcome was, but it sounded like the ladies had given their bank account numbers to an unknown, risky business. Scammers claiming they're with investment groups are scamming not only seniors or vulnerable folks but young, well-educated people who believe they're investing hundreds of thousands of dollars to companies, claiming they're building condos, tourist resorts, developments of all sorts. No. In fact, in one incident the associate for the company stole the money and was long gone, unable to be charged with fraud. Very saddened to hear of a wife, when her husband was away at his work site, invested a large amount of funds in a company that did not even exist. Another incident: folks invested in a tourist development at one of our national parks that never got off the ground, lost funds never to be refunded. Scammers even attack our small local marketplaces for just at twenty-dollar item. How low can they get? Thank God no account numbers were exchanged. The popular scam at present is the call from a grandchild needing bail money. Grandpa falls for this scam, even though Gramma says it's a scam.

Businesses, town offices, sports groups, churches are all being targeted. Then there's the daily scam phone calls using local phone numbers and store business names, so automatically we pick up the receiver but once again, a scammer. What is very hurtful is when one knows of a friend of a friend who fell into a scam situation. When will it end? Technology so advanced to the authorities, government, and fraud security systems are having difficult times to put a stop to all this dishonesty and corruption.

Upon completion of this section on scammers, just as I have written earlier about young folks getting scammed and trapped is on the rise, on the news is talk about why young people and children are at a higher risk of being scammed, because they are online more so. Not that they have large sums of money to send to scammers but all amounts are accepted. Children, teens, and young adults, beware of your surroundings and your unknown contacts. Look up off the screen once in a while and listen to what's going on around you.

Time with no limit will heal the pain and regain one's healthy, happy state of mind. I feel in my heart I'm going to be there shortly, once this book is published. Then to relax and enjoy the next retirement until the next book I have started, which is a joyous, happy book. I'm going back to enjoy my country way of life and all of God's natural creations. Care to join me for friendship or companionship? No sooner said, book #2 has begun, notes been made and placed in a binder. This time no secret withheld, in the book "*Lost in Lundbreck*".

No sympathy necessary, but thank you for all your concerns for my wellness. I have overcome my mistake of the risk I had taken. I jumped over the hurdles to the finish line to a stronger and wiser person that I didn't know I had in me. Writing this was a godsend. Many an author have written to get through grieving, just exactly as I have and this has made me more aware of what is really taking place in this modern-day era. I have found my happy place, so all is good within my body, mind, and soul. With that being said, my next book will be a joy to read. Stay tuned. I can hardly wait until the completion of *Lost in Lundbreck* is placed on the store bookshelves and libraries. Between the sunrises and sunsets, enjoy your time, make the most of each day, until we meet again.

Secrets

Tell me no secrets and I will tell you no lies. Are they secrets or must I lie to keep a secret? I believe throughout our lifetime we have secrets we may hold onto forever or we reveal the secret from the hidden closet when the timing is right or when the secret becomes reality. Call them little white lies, which can be very harmful and cause sadness and shame. Secrets give meaning and understanding when surfaced and why they were hidden and kept away from truth. Then once known and shared, the reasoning should be dealt with. I believe even the few secrets I have held inside did not damper my honesty but it sure made it uncomfortable holding onto something in that mind that never should have been there in the first place. Let go of those secrets, we have nothing to hide, and once true, honesty will be brighter.

I must confess the largest sinful secret I'm committing is now while I'm writing this book, reasons why, which will all be revealed once the book is published.

In all honesty I told everyone I'm writing a book but since my first thought of compiling notes for my book, the story has been kept a secret. Many have asked of the book, but no one knows the title, nor the content for a story or the cover or the end. It is my surprise secret until the book is completed. Later I want to rid my mind of this secret lie so I will not be haunted for the rest of my life. In due time I want to feel relieved of the embarrassing and disrespectful situation. Especially to my dearest family members who are my greatest support please forgive me for this it will never happen again. I hope and pray my family and friends will see the reasoning behind it all, it was all temporary, and I managed through this stressful time keeping the secret within. I so wanted so many times to tell the world and follow my journey but just wanted all to be said with pen on paper. To all the readers of my book, I hope this story is educational, inspirational, and righteous.

Some shameful things we feel might destroy what our years of love and trust have built, so afraid of what others might think when our secrets are revealed. We've hidden guilt, should have shared them from the start, those secrets we felt needed keeping out of view. They might have understood why we hid them, only then showing them apart of ourselves.

Thank you to the special people in my life who have listened without judgment, helped without conditions, understood with empathy, and loved me no matter what.

If you live in the past, you are depressed.

If you live in the future, you are anxious.

If you live in the present, you are at peace.

Never focus on the noise that surrounds you.

CHAPTER 8
Confessions

The universe is saying to you today, you may find others questioning or judging you and your choices but understand that this is their opinion and viewpoint and this may be true for them, but it is not your truth. Listen to your own heart and choose what is right for you. Choose to do what makes your heart sing.

Just let them, whomever they may be, be wrong about you. You know who you are. They can say whatever they want but what's that going to change? You are still you and another person cannot change that, just let them be wrong. Prove to yourself what is right or wrong.

No matter what you do, someone will always talk about you, someone will always question your judgment. Someone will always doubt you. Just smile and make choices you can live with.

You don't have to be positive all the time. It's perfectly OK to feel sad, angry, scared, or anxious. Having feelings doesn't make you a negative person. It makes you human.

My Spiritual Apology

Once this book is published, I owe many apologies to family, friends, and acquaintances.

Only one heartfelt apology, and one given several times, will be given to my only true love in my lifetime, spoken with many of tears for my late husband, Ken McKellar. Please accept my deepest apology for the issue that was imposed upon myself at the saddest point in my life. With empty feelings, I reached out for attention that comforted me. What was I thinking? I guess my mind was totally foggy and weak to see right from wrong. This would not have ever, I mean ever, happened with Ken at my side. It took a few months until I realized I needed to rectify the dramatic situation, and I did. I gave my head a shake cleared those negative thoughts and regrouped to my normal mindset. Back to myself, "I Will Survive" and carry on with my new journey in a happy, healthy way. I'm as strong as I once was.

While writing my apology I played "For the Good Times" by Kris Kristofferson, which was Ken's favourite song. The words reflected exactly how I felt.

Rest in peace with the music playing always:

Ken: March 29, 2024

Kris: September 28, 2024

Please, Lord, forgive me for I have sinned. I have repeated ten Our Fathers and five Hail Marys. In the name of the Father, the Son, and the Holy Spirit. Amen.

Today was quite intense, for as this book is nearing completion, I glanced up from pen and paper to give my eyes a rest and to refocus. Looking out the window, there on the tree branch, two doves roosting side by side, preening themselves and each other, pecking like they were kissing, cuddling close to touch each other. Hence the name love doves. They flew away together in unity.

We can learn from nature and recognize only small gestures can mean so much to make love grow now and forever.

As I continued to write this ending, I listened to tunes like "It's Who You Love" by Don Williams.

This modern world we live in is a sad state of affairs. Everyone wants what isn't theirs. We race for money and success in search of happiness. We turn out the lights and go upstairs. My best days were spent with my husband, Ken, of forty-five years. Nothing or no one can replace that wonderful time we had together. Memories of the good times, I will hold in my heart always and forever.

"For the Good Times" by Andy Williams—another great tune.

Knowing True Love

True love is a kind of love that lasts, unconditional love goes back to play. Who once said love is when somebody else is hurt, they sing a song that only you can hear? What that means is when you're in love, it's not because they're attractive, it's not because they have money or a nice car, it's because there is something in them you can no longer do without. People might not understand what you see but for you they are the most beautiful person in the world, they are the most interesting mind you've ever encountered, they're the person you want to be with every single day. Their conversations light you up, their laugh makes you smile, their touch makes you feel cherished and safe. Love is not finding the most suitable person, love is not a strategic conquest. Love is finding that somebody whose heart sings that song straight to your heart. If you find and have this kind of love, may it last forever.

True love, story ending.

All stories have a beginning and an ending. They may end in sadness or happiness. They may leave one in suspense till the next book in a series is written. They may leave you in a mystical state of mind, or a reality that is not immediately apparent to the senses or the mind. Fictional stories may find oneself adding facts to fill in the blanks. Humorous stories create laughter and joy, start to finish, and are good to enlighten those dark days. With my book, my dear readers, I'm hoping you read soulful love, a union of two souls, a meeting of heart, mind, and spirit. Be thankful for yesterday, be grateful for today, and be hopeful for tomorrow. I, Ettie, greatly need to end this on a happy note. Compassionate tears and heartfelt emotions, enjoy life to the fullest.

Dearest Ken,

"I can't promise that I'll be here for the rest of your life, but I can promise that I will love you for the rest of mine."

—Rosanna B. Lundberg

"Sometimes you will never know the value of a moment until it becomes a memory."

—Dr. Seuss

I choose to love you in silence …
For in silence I find no rejection,

I choose to love you in loneliness …
For loneliness no one owns you but me,

I choose to adore you from a distance …
For distance will shield me from pain,

I choose to kiss you in the wind …
For the wind is gentler than my lips,

I choose to hold you in my dreams …
For in my dreams you have no end.

—Rumi

Ethel McKellar

"Forever and Ever, Amen" by Randy Travis

I truly cherished our, Love, Ken and I shared for forty-five years.

Printed in Canada